# Contents

© 1988 by EVAN-MOOR CORP.

Folded Paper Projects

# Fish

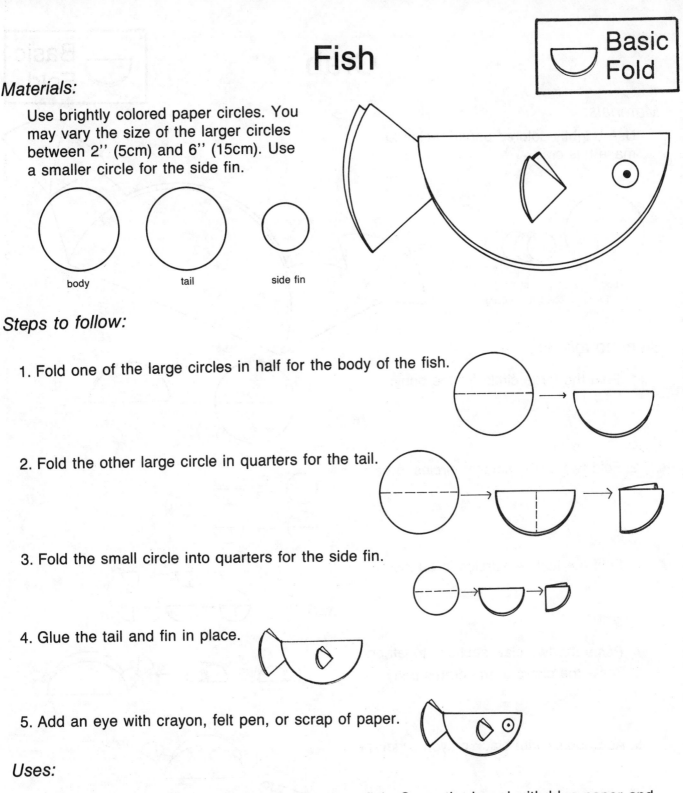

## Materials:

Use brightly colored paper circles. You may vary the size of the larger circles between 2'' (5cm) and 6'' (15cm). Use a smaller circle for the side fin.

body        tail        side fin

## Steps to follow:

1. Fold one of the large circles in half for the body of the fish.

2. Fold the other large circle in quarters for the tail.

3. Fold the small circle into quarters for the side fin.

4. Glue the tail and fin in place.

5. Add an eye with crayon, felt pen, or scrap of paper.

## Uses:

- Create a colorful bulletin board with these fish. Cover the board with blue paper and arrange the fish. Let students make the fish from several bright colors of paper. Use this "school of fish" to reinforce concepts your class is studying.

  ordinals          contractions
  color words       compound words

- Students now create dioramas using several of these fish. Paint the inside of a shoebox blue and suspend the fish from threads. Cut plants from green paper to glue along the sides and back of the box. Smear white glue diluted with water on the bottom of the diorama. Sprinkle sand over the wet glue.

Folded Paper Projects

# Crab

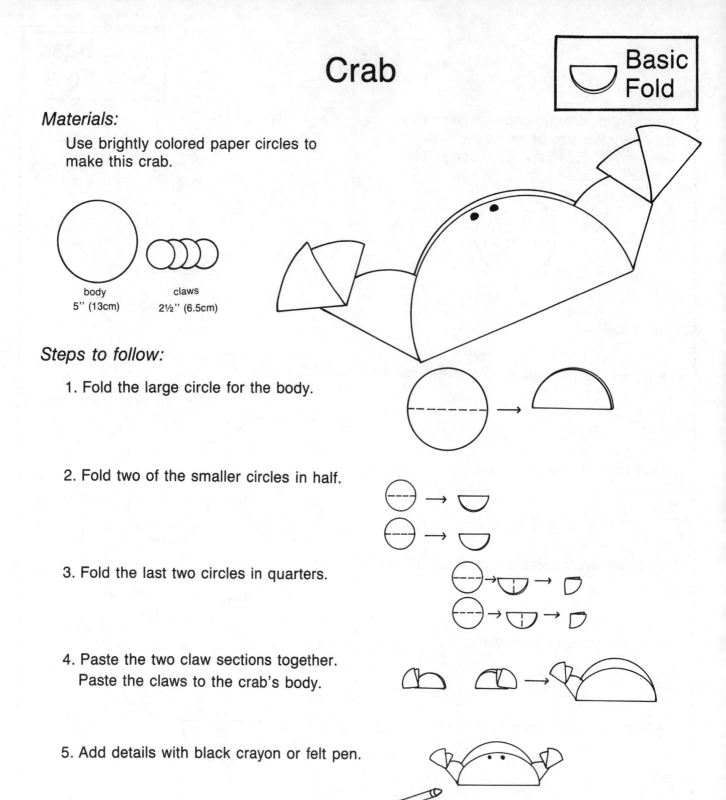

## Materials:

Use brightly colored paper circles to make this crab.

body
5'' (13cm)

claws
2½'' (6.5cm)

## Steps to follow:

1. Fold the large circle for the body.

2. Fold two of the smaller circles in half.

3. Fold the last two circles in quarters.

4. Paste the two claw sections together. Paste the claws to the crab's body.

5. Add details with black crayon or felt pen.

## Uses:

- These crabs create a bright border for a bulletin board that displays stories about the seashore.
- Paste a crab to a piece of 9'' x 12'' (22.8 x 30.5cm) blue construction paper. Use scraps of paper or crayon to create an underwater scene.
- Tape a line of crabs in your windows. Put eyes on both the front and the back. Cut green tissue paper and tape it (twisting and bending) between and around the crabs for kelp.

Folded Paper Projects

# Quail

## Materials:

Use one paper circle and a few scraps of construction paper to make this quail.

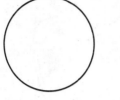

The size of the circle is up to you. You may want to make them in several sizes.

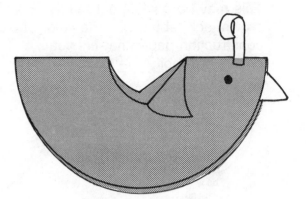

## Steps to follow:

1. Fold the circle in half.

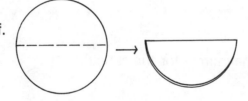

2. Cut a curved wing. Make a slit along the fold.

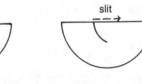

3. Paste a scrap on the inside of the circle for the beak. Add a curled strip for the top knot.

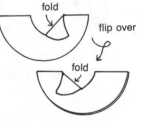

4. Add an eye with black crayon or felt pen.

## Uses:

- Make a whole family of quail to display in your room.
- Older students enjoy coloring the quail markings realistically.

Folded Paper Projects

# Rabbit

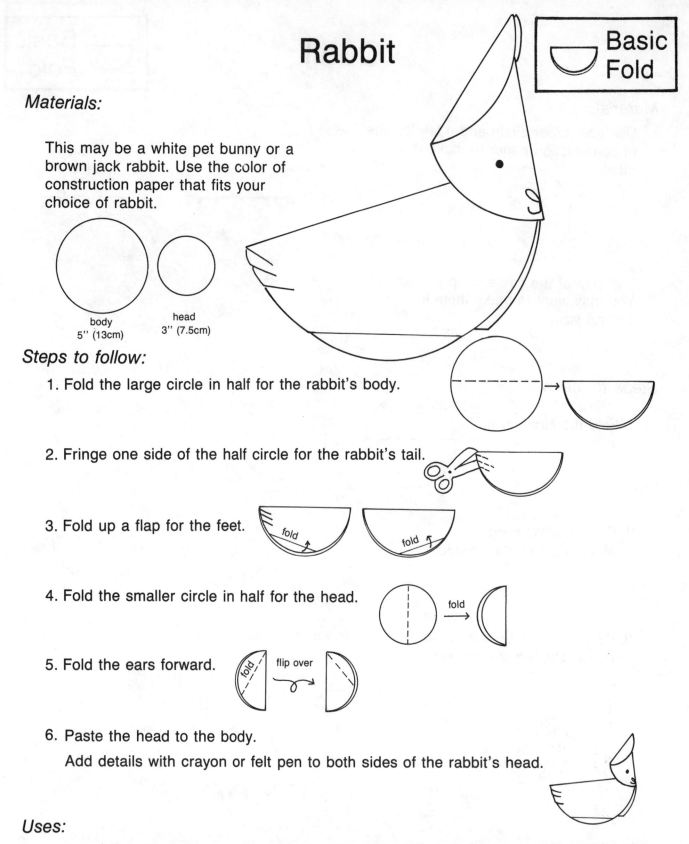

**Basic Fold**

## Materials:

This may be a white pet bunny or a brown jack rabbit. Use the color of construction paper that fits your choice of rabbit.

body
5'' (13cm)

head
3'' (7.5cm)

## Steps to follow:

1. Fold the large circle in half for the rabbit's body.

2. Fringe one side of the half circle for the rabbit's tail.

3. Fold up a flap for the feet.

   fold        fold

4. Fold the smaller circle in half for the head.

   fold

5. Fold the ears forward.

   fold   flip over

6. Paste the head to the body.

   Add details with crayon or felt pen to both sides of the rabbit's head.

## Uses:

- Paste the rabbits feet to a larger piece of construction paper and invite students to retell the story of little Peter Rabbit scurrying through Mr. McGregor's garden.
- Cut out a pair of red wings from construction paper and paste to the rabbit. Now you have a storytelling prop to use along with the story — *The Rabbit Who Wanted Red Wings*.

6

# Caterpillar

**Materials:**

Use a strip of 2'' x 5'' (5 x 13cm) paper. Color is optional. Students may wish to use white paper and add stripes and dots to create their own unusual species of caterpillar.

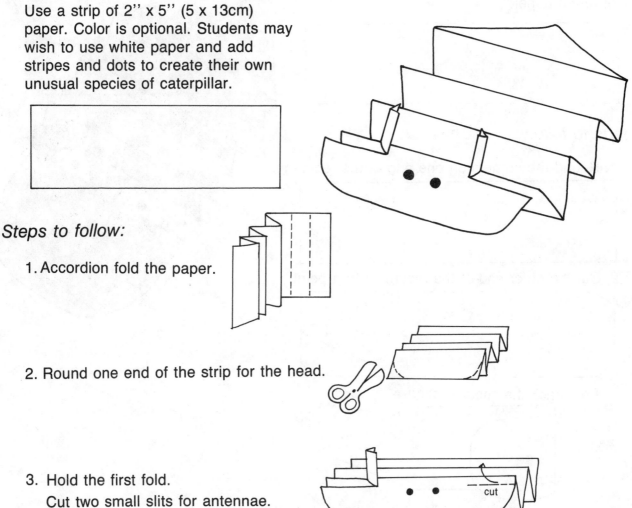

**Steps to follow:**

1. Accordion fold the paper.

2. Round one end of the strip for the head.

3. Hold the first fold.
   Cut two small slits for antennae.
   Fold them up. Add eyes with felt pen, paper scraps, or black beans.

   cut

4. Cut the last segment to a point.

**Uses:**

- Pin these little friends to large leaves on a bulletin board. Use this board to list science facts about caterpillars or as a place to display student poems and short stories about nature.
- Glue caterpillars to student's individual paper gardens. Cut three dimensional flowers and leaves from construction paper.
- Tape each student's caterpillar to his/her shoulder as a ''listening companion'' for the day.

# Alligator

*Materials:*

Use a 9'' x 3'' (22.8 x 7.5cm) rectangle
of green paper.

*Steps to follow:*

1. Round the corners on one end of the rectangle.

2. Cut the other end of the rectangle to a point.

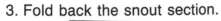

3. Fold back the snout section.

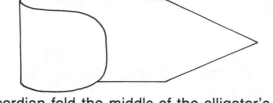

4. Accordian fold the middle of the alligator's body.

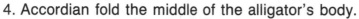

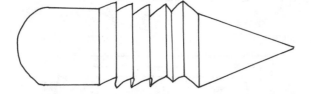

5. Add facial details with black crayon or felt pen.

*Uses:*

- Pin these alligator's all around the bulletin board. Display student work in the center and add a caption that reads "Gator Greats".
- Paste the tail and base of alligator's snout to blue paper. The mouth of the alligator must still open up. Cut out a paper fish and paste it on the blue paper under alligator's snout.

Folded Paper Projects

# Angel

**Materials:**

Use a 9'' x 3'' (22.8 x 7.5cm) rectangle of paper.

Reproduce the body parts patterns on this page.

**Steps to follow:**

1. Accordian fold the rectangle in ¾'' (2cm) segments. Pinch the folds together and staple the top half.

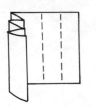

2. Paste on the body parts.

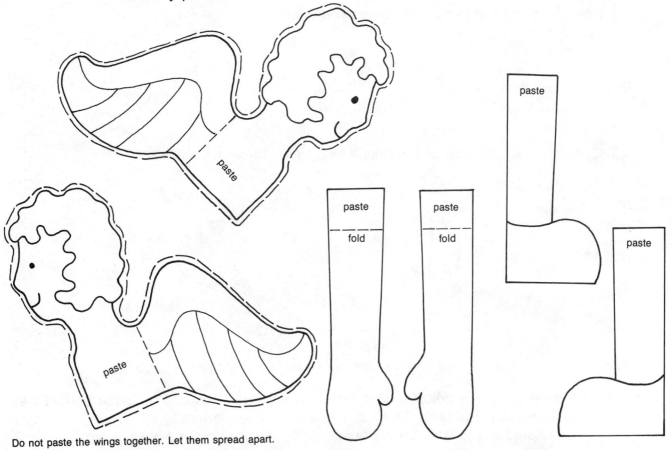

Do not paste the wings together. Let them spread apart.

9

Folded Paper Projects

# Raindrop

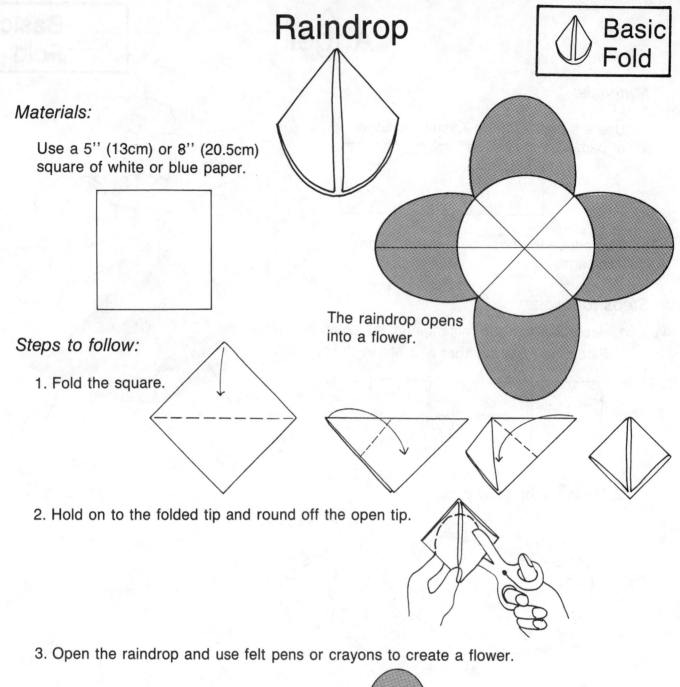
**Materials:**

Use a 5'' (13cm) or 8'' (20.5cm) square of white or blue paper.

The raindrop opens into a flower.

**Steps to follow:**

1. Fold the square.

2. Hold on to the folded tip and round off the open tip.

3. Open the raindrop and use felt pens or crayons to create a flower.

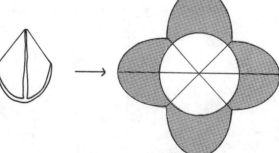

**Uses:**

- Pin the raindrops below a huge cloud on a bulletin board. This is the perfect way to illustrate the phrase, ''April showers bring May flowers.''
- Invite students to write poetry about spring inside the raindrops.

# Ladybug

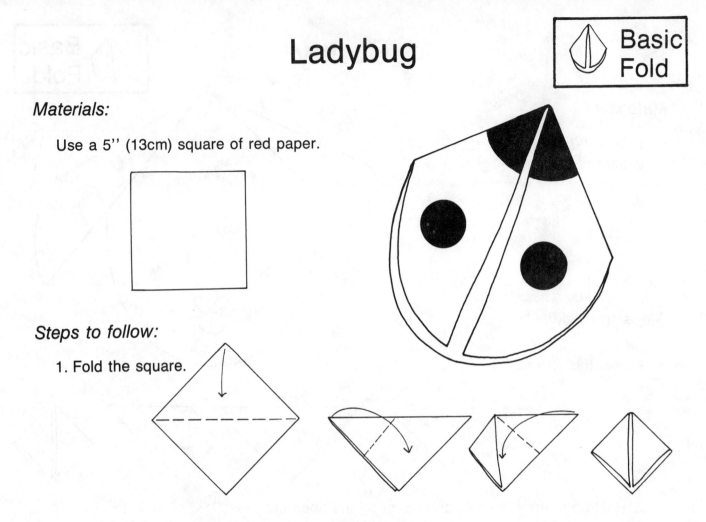

Basic Fold

## Materials:

Use a 5'' (13cm) square of red paper.

## Steps to follow:

1. Fold the square.

2. Hold on to the folded tip and round off the open tip.

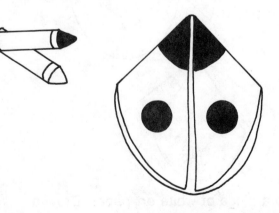

3. Add details with felt pen or crayon.

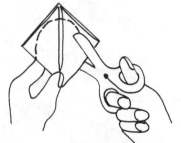

## Uses:

- Make a large tree on the bulletin board. Pin ladybugs on the branches.
- Paste a ladybug on the front of an invitation to parents to visit the classroom.

11

# Bunny

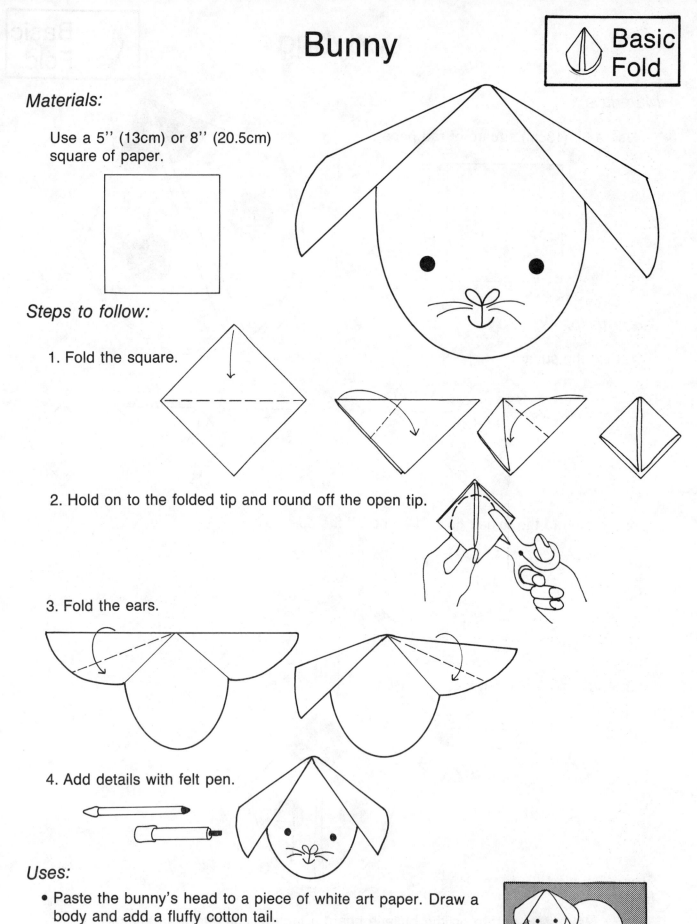

**Basic Fold**

## Materials:

Use a 5'' (13cm) or 8'' (20.5cm) square of paper.

## Steps to follow:

1. Fold the square.

2. Hold on to the folded tip and round off the open tip.

3. Fold the ears.

4. Add details with felt pen.

## Uses:

- Paste the bunny's head to a piece of white art paper. Draw a body and add a fluffy cotton tail.
- Unfold bunny's head and write a simple message or couplet. Send it home as an Easter card.

12

# Dutch Girl

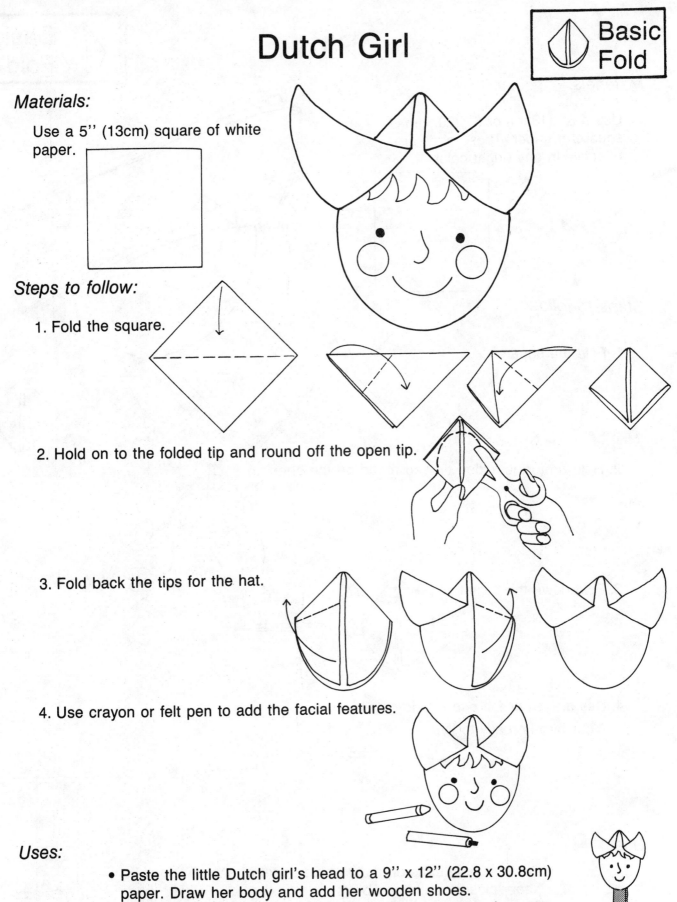

*Materials:*

Use a 5'' (13cm) square of white paper.

*Steps to follow:*

1. Fold the square.

2. Hold on to the folded tip and round off the open tip.

3. Fold back the tips for the hat.

4. Use crayon or felt pen to add the facial features.

*Uses:*

- Paste the little Dutch girl's head to a 9'' x 12'' (22.8 x 30.8cm) paper. Draw her body and add her wooden shoes.
- Glue the little Dutch girl's head to a straw or tongue depressor to make a stick puppet.

13

# Bird

## Materials:

Use a 5'' (13cm) or 8'' (20.5cm) square of paper. These birds are effective in any bright color.

## Steps to follow:

1. Fold the square.

2. Hold on to the folded tip and round off the open tip.

3. Fold down the center.

4. Use crayon or felt pen to add details.
   Your bird is ready to fly.

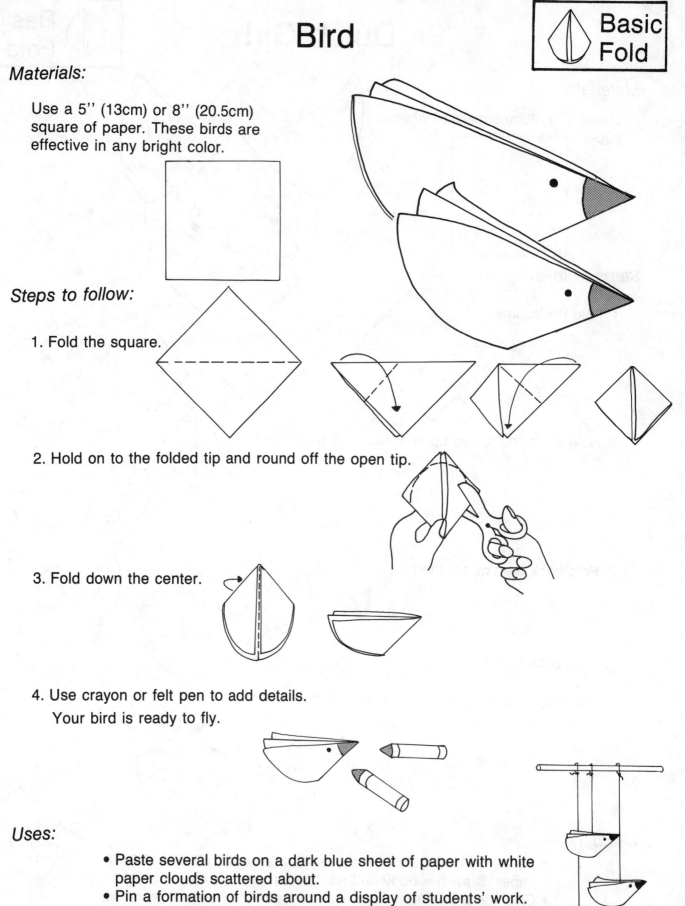

## Uses:

- Paste several birds on a dark blue sheet of paper with white paper clouds scattered about.
- Pin a formation of birds around a display of students' work. Use the caption, "We flock to good work."
- Suspend several of the birds from strings to create a mobile.

     Folded Paper Projects

# Fish

**Materials:**

Use a 5'' (13cm) or 8'' (20.5cm) square of brightly colored paper.

**Steps to follow:**

1. Fold the square.
   Hold on to the folded tip and round off the open tip.

2. Fold back the fins.

3. Reverse the cut off tip of paper and paste it onto the fish as a tail.

4. Add an eye with felt pen or crayon. You may also add decorative polka-dots and stripes.

**Uses:**

- Add these colorful fish to an underwater bulletin board scene. Arrange a whole school across the board. Pin green twisted tissue paper across the bottom as kelp.
- Make the fish in a larger version (10'' [25.5cm] square). Hang them from the light fixtures with string.

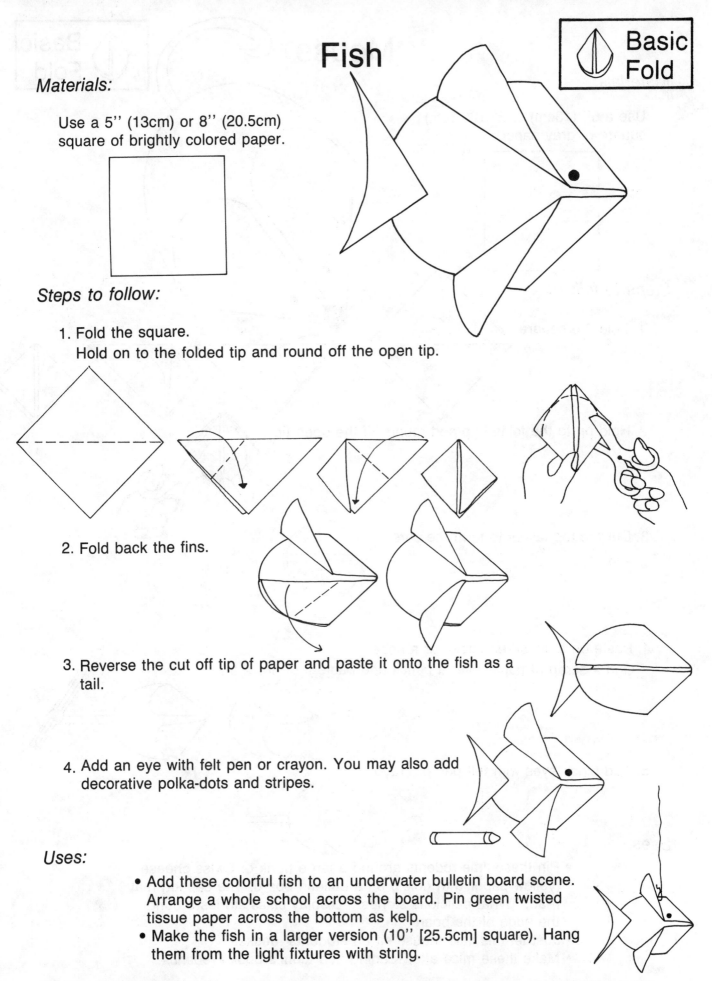

# Mouse

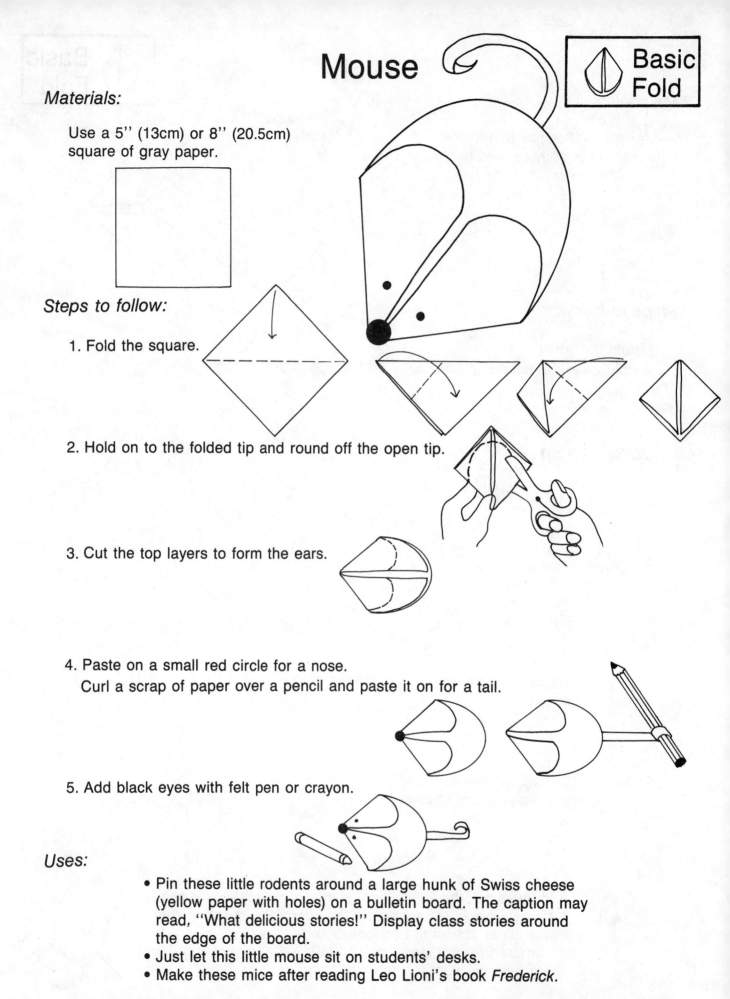

**Materials:**

Use a 5'' (13cm) or 8'' (20.5cm)
square of gray paper.

**Steps to follow:**

1. Fold the square.

2. Hold on to the folded tip and round off the open tip.

3. Cut the top layers to form the ears.

4. Paste on a small red circle for a nose.
   Curl a scrap of paper over a pencil and paste it on for a tail.

5. Add black eyes with felt pen or crayon.

**Uses:**

- Pin these little rodents around a large hunk of Swiss cheese (yellow paper with holes) on a bulletin board. The caption may read, ''What delicious stories!'' Display class stories around the edge of the board.
- Just let this little mouse sit on students' desks.
- Make these mice after reading Leo Lioni's book *Frederick*.

16

# Pig

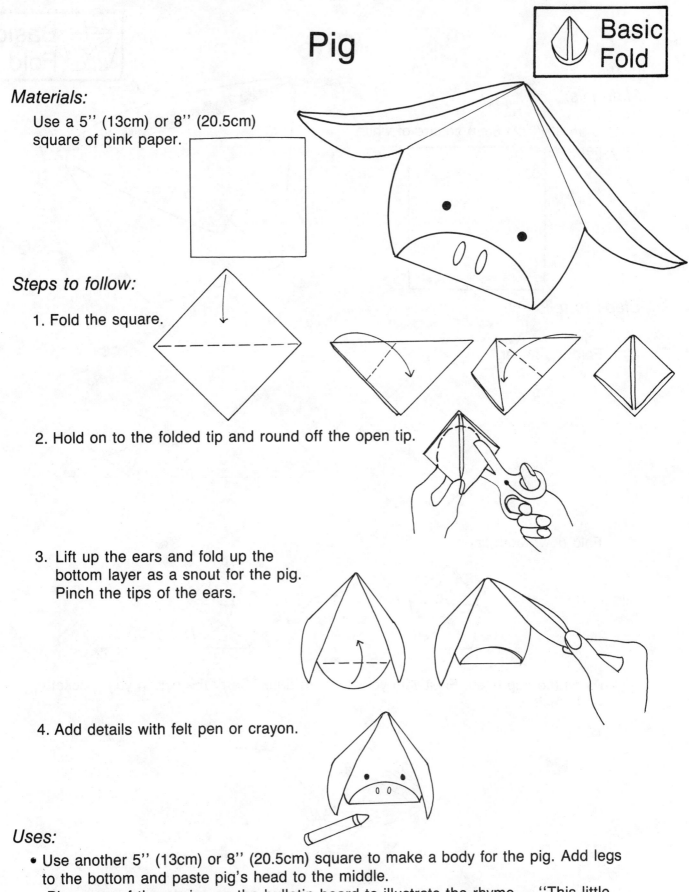

**Materials:**

Use a 5'' (13cm) or 8'' (20.5cm) square of pink paper.

**Steps to follow:**

1. Fold the square.

2. Hold on to the folded tip and round off the open tip.

3. Lift up the ears and fold up the bottom layer as a snout for the pig. Pinch the tips of the ears.

4. Add details with felt pen or crayon.

**Uses:**

- Use another 5'' (13cm) or 8'' (20.5cm) square to make a body for the pig. Add legs to the bottom and paste pig's head to the middle.
- Pin a row of these pigs on the bulletin board to illustrate the rhyme — "This little piggie went to market."
- Dress the pig as the character Garth in the books by Mary Rayner (*Mr. & Mrs. Pig's Evening Out; Garth and the Ice Cream Lady*).

# Cup

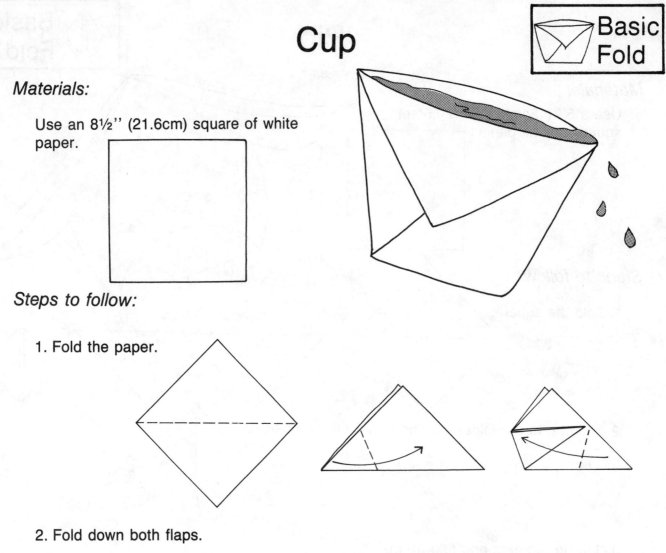

## Materials:

Use an 8½'' (21.6cm) square of white paper.

## Steps to follow:

1. Fold the paper.

2. Fold down both flaps.

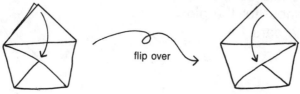

flip over

3. Pinch the cup open. Fill it with your favorite drink. Carry the cup in your pocket while hiking.

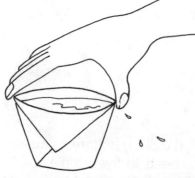

## Uses:

- Make the cup in a larger version and fill it with popcorn for a party.
- Use these cups as disposable containers when demonstrating color–mixing principles.

Folded Paper Projects

# Hat

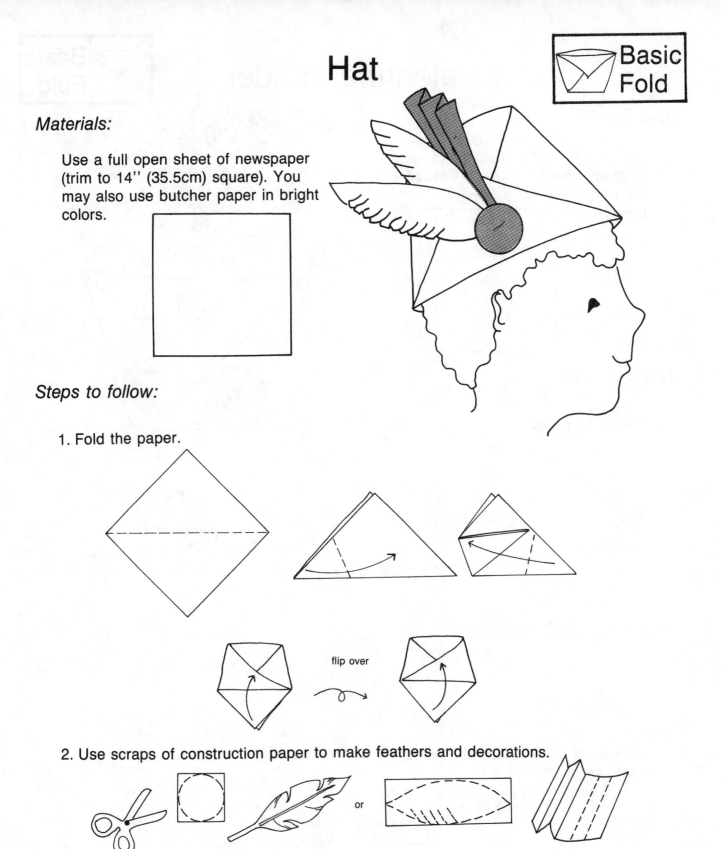

**Materials:**

Use a full open sheet of newspaper (trim to 14'' (35.5cm) square). You may also use butcher paper in bright colors.

**Steps to follow:**

1. Fold the paper.

flip over

2. Use scraps of construction paper to make feathers and decorations.

or

**Uses:**

- Let students make their own hats to wear while you recite *Drummer Hoff* by Ed Emberly.
- Use this opportunity to enjoy a march by John Phillip Sousa. Everyone wears their colorful hat and marches around the room.
- Wear the hat sideways to celebrate George Washington's birthday.

Folded Paper Projects

# Valentine Holder

**Materials:**

Use an 18'' (45.7cm) square of
butcher paper in white, pink or red.
(You may also use a sheet of
newsprint.)

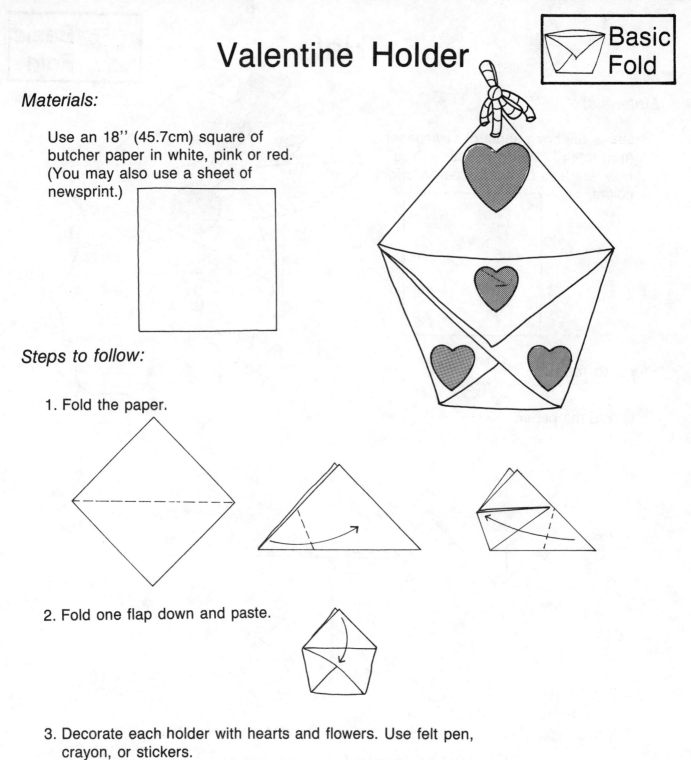

**Steps to follow:**

1. Fold the paper.

2. Fold one flap down and paste.

3. Decorate each holder with hearts and flowers. Use felt pen,
   crayon, or stickers.

**Uses:**

- Use this basic fold as a May basket. Fill it with flowers and
  hang it on a friend's door on May 1st.
- This project may be used as a ''note holder'' that students
  can make for their mothers for Mother's Day. Tie a bow to the
  top of the holder.

           Folded Paper Projects

# Turtle

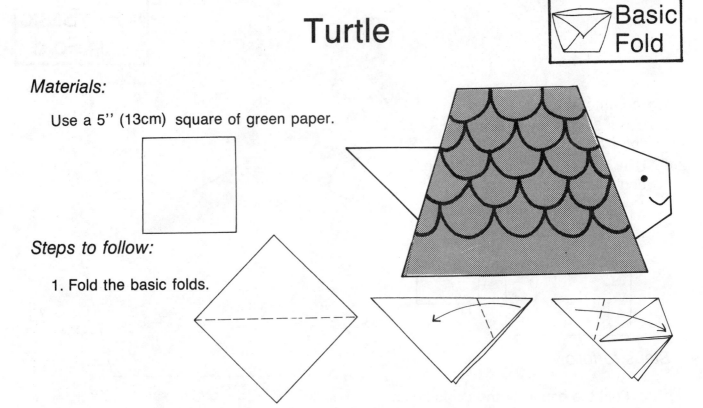
*Materials:*

Use a 5'' (13cm) square of green paper.

*Steps to follow:*

1. Fold the basic folds.

2. Turn up the two points. Press them under the two flaps.

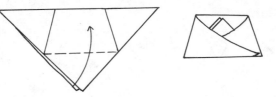

3. Fold back one tip for the turtle's tail. Then fold back the other tip.
   Fold back the point for the turtle's head.

flip over

4. Add an eye and a smile plus texture lines on the shell with crayon or felt pen.

*Uses:*

• Paste turtle to a sheet of construction paper. Invite students to write facts about turtles. Paste the writing paper on the back of the construction paper.
• Make two turtles: one facing left and one facing right. Paste them to a sheet of construction paper. Paste cartoon bubbles above their heads. What does one turtle say to another?

# Dog

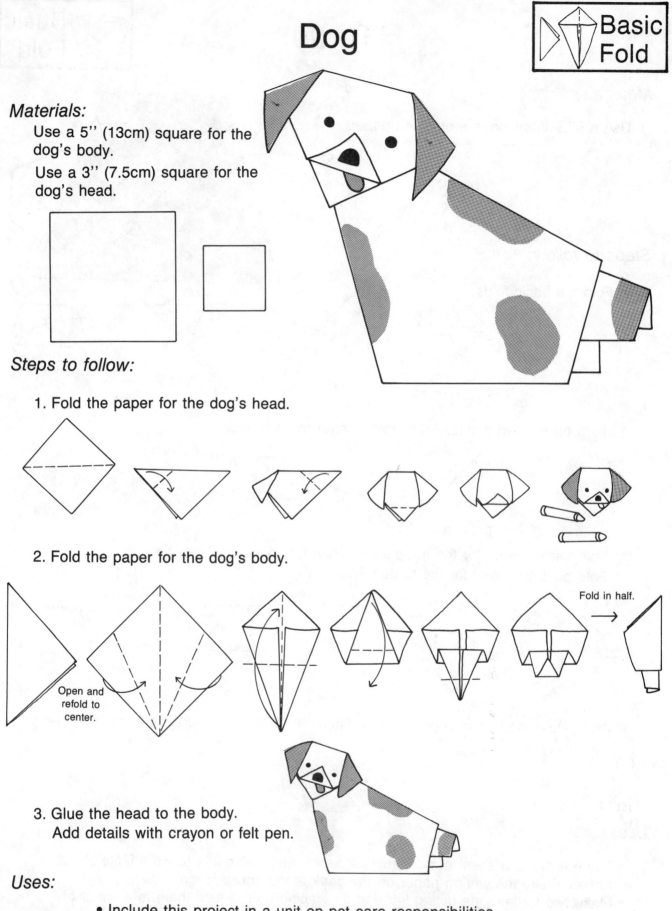

## Materials:

Use a 5'' (13cm) square for the dog's body.

Use a 3'' (7.5cm) square for the dog's head.

## Steps to follow:

1. Fold the paper for the dog's head.

2. Fold the paper for the dog's body.

Open and refold to center.

Fold in half.

3. Glue the head to the body.
   Add details with crayon or felt pen.

## Uses:

- Include this project in a unit on pet care responsibilities.
- Share the series of books by Eric Hill about Spot with your students.

# Raccoon

**Materials:**

Use a 7'' (18cm) gray square for raccoon's body.
Use a 3'' (7.5cm) gray square for raccoon's head.

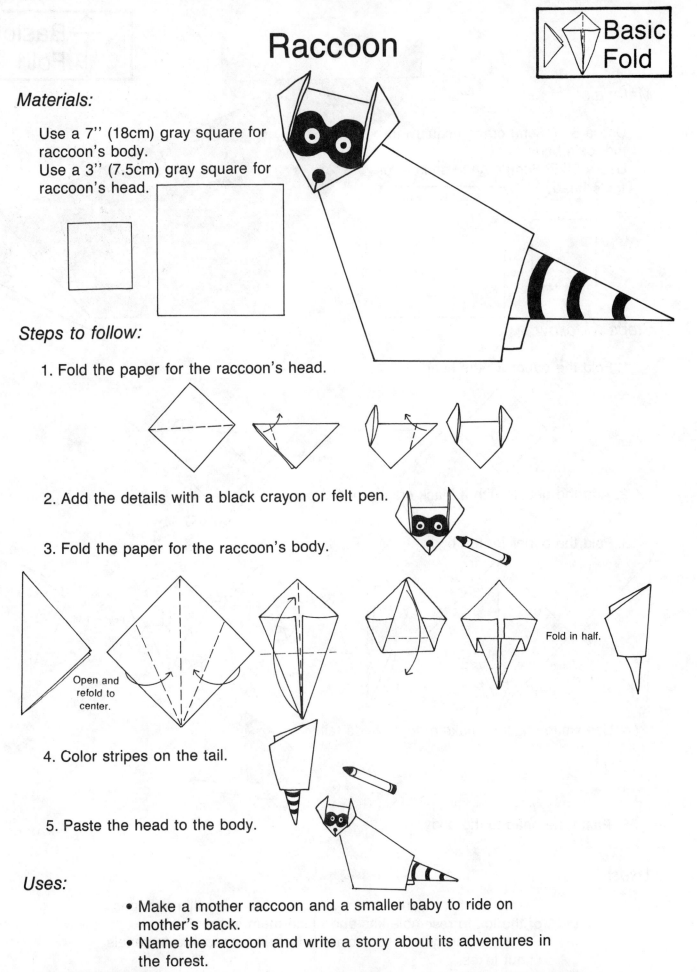

**Steps to follow:**

1. Fold the paper for the raccoon's head.

2. Add the details with a black crayon or felt pen.

3. Fold the paper for the raccoon's body.

Open and refold to center.

Fold in half.

4. Color stripes on the tail.

5. Paste the head to the body.

**Uses:**

- Make a mother raccoon and a smaller baby to ride on mother's back.
- Name the raccoon and write a story about its adventures in the forest.

Folded Paper Projects

# Fox

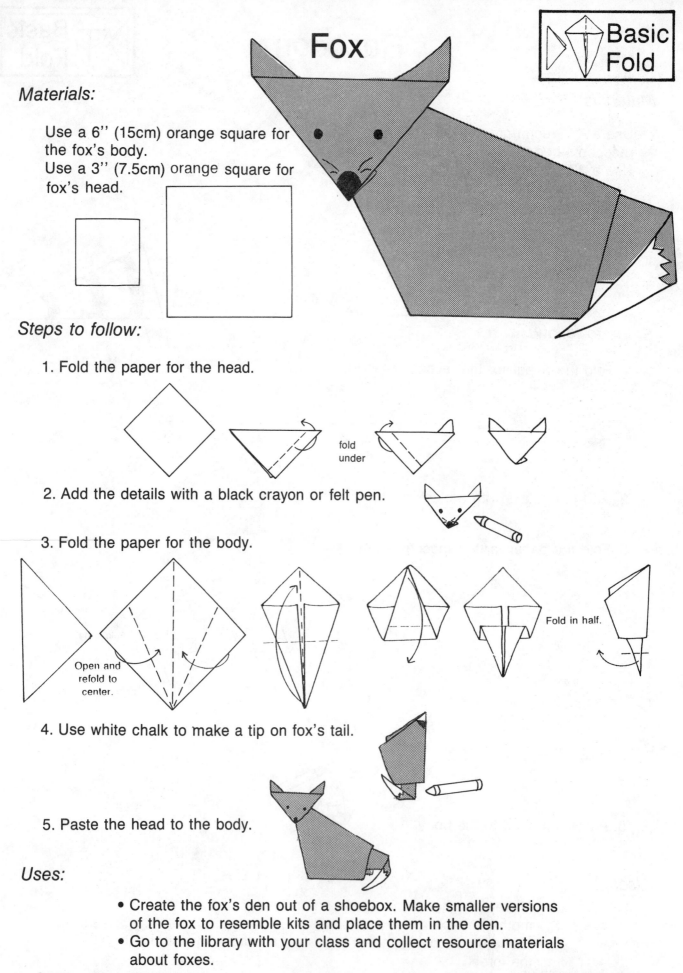

**Basic Fold**

**Materials:**

Use a 6'' (15cm) orange square for the fox's body.
Use a 3'' (7.5cm) orange square for fox's head.

**Steps to follow:**

1. Fold the paper for the head.

fold under

2. Add the details with a black crayon or felt pen.

3. Fold the paper for the body.

Open and refold to center.

Fold in half.

4. Use white chalk to make a tip on fox's tail.

5. Paste the head to the body.

**Uses:**

- Create the fox's den out of a shoebox. Make smaller versions of the fox to resemble kits and place them in the den.
- Go to the library with your class and collect resource materials about foxes.

Folded Paper Projects

# House

Basic Fold

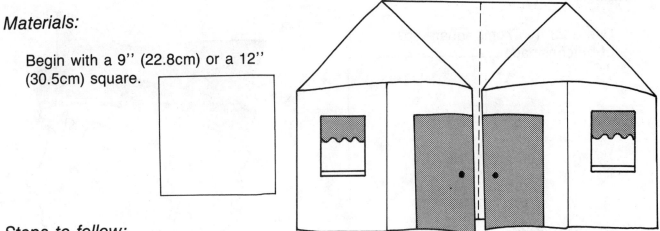

## Materials:

Begin with a 9'' (22.8cm) or a 12'' (30.5cm) square.

## Steps to follow:

### 1. Fold the paper.

Open up and refold.

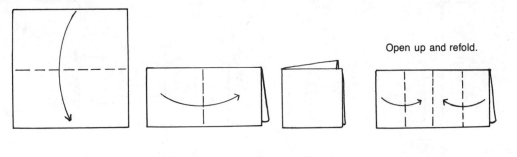

Fold down corners.

Open outside flaps.

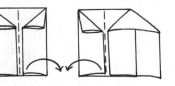

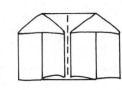

Open and close the doors to peek inside the house.

### 2. Add details with crayon or felt pen.

outside

inside

## Uses:

- This project may be used as an invitation to send to parents for open house. Have students write the information inside the folded area.
- Let students draw their family inside the house as a part of a class unit on families. Pin the completed houses to a bulletin board to create a neighborhood map. Draw streets with a felt pen.
- Read *Oh, Were They Ever Happy* by Peter Spier. Your class will enjoy the drama of watching children paint their house while their parents are away for the afternoon.

Folded Paper Projects

# Hat

*Materials:*

Use a 22'' (55.7 cm) square sheet
of butcher paper.

*Steps to follow:*

1. Fold the basic folds.

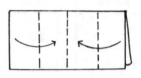

Open up and refold.

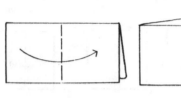

Fold down corners.

Open outside flaps.

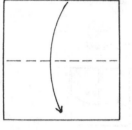

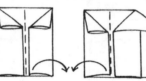

2. Flip the paper over. Bend the side flaps back. Roll up twice from the bottom.

 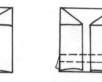 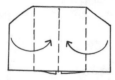 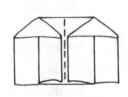 

Flip the paper over
and repeat the folds
on the back layer.

3. Open the hat and push in the top.

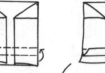

*Uses:*

- Make "lots of hats" and let the class retell the story of *The 500 Hats of Bartholomew Cubbins* by Dr. Seuss. Add plumes and feathers.
- Decorate one of these hats as a special birthday surprise for your students to wear on their special day.

26

# Frilled Lizard

*Materials:*

Use a 6'' (15cm) square of paper.
Typing or copy machine paper is a
good weight.

*Steps to follow:*

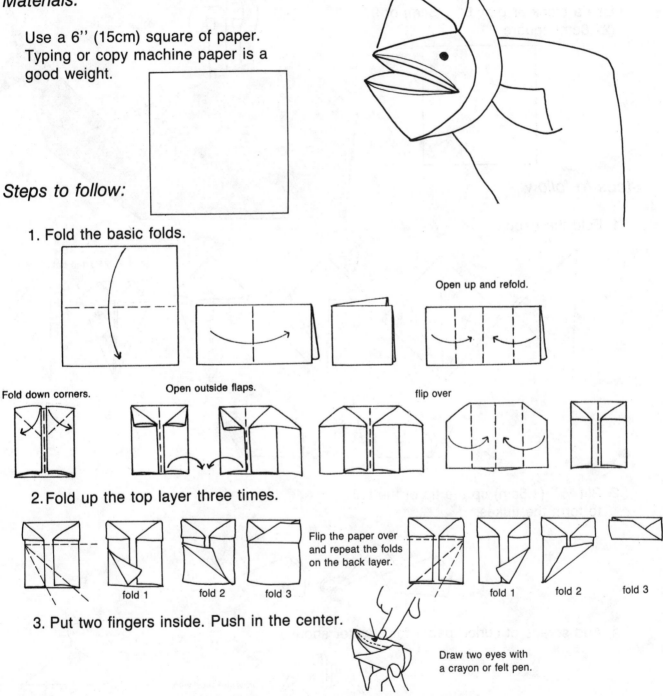

1. Fold the basic folds.

Open up and refold.

Fold down corners.    Open outside flaps.    flip over

2. Fold up the top layer three times.

fold 1    fold 2    fold 3

Flip the paper over
and repeat the folds
on the back layer.

fold 1    fold 2    fold 3

3. Put two fingers inside. Push in the center.

Draw two eyes with
a crayon or felt pen.

4. Put your fingers inside the points and let the lizard open and close his mouth.

*Uses:*

- Let children chant:
  "I'm frilled as frilled can be
  That someone like you is friends with me."
- Encourage students to tell where the "frilled lizard" is from
  and what he likes best for dinner.

# Whale

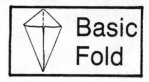
### Materials:

Use a black or gray 6'' (15cm) or 9'' (22.8cm) square.

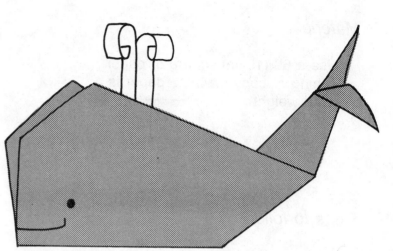

### Steps to follow:

1. Fold the paper.

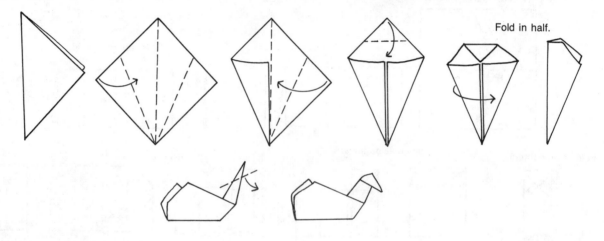

Fold in half.

2. Slit ½'' (1.5cm) up the tip of the tail to form the flukes.

3. Add scraps of curled paper for a water spout.

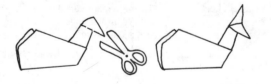

Draw the face with crayon or felt pen.

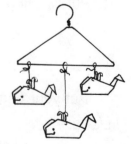

### Uses:

- Paste several of the whales to a blue background and discuss their winter migration habits.
- Make a whale mobile. Hang whales in several sizes from strings on a wire coat hanger.

28    Folded Paper Projects

# Snail

**Materials:**

Use a 6'' (15cm) square of white paper.

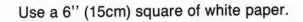

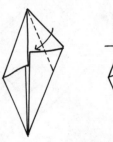

**Steps to follow:**

1. Fold the paper.

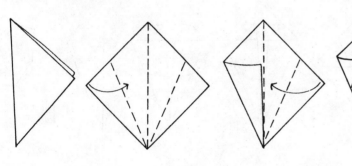

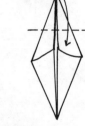

Fold closed.

Slit ½'' (1.5cm) on fold. Bend top layer forward.

push in

Turn on the side.

2. Add details with crayon or felt pen.

**Uses:**

- Cut a large leaf from green paper and paste the snail to it.
- Read *The Snail's Spell* by Joanne Ryder.

        Folded Paper Projects

# Swan

*Materials:*

Use a 6'' (15cm) square piece of white paper.

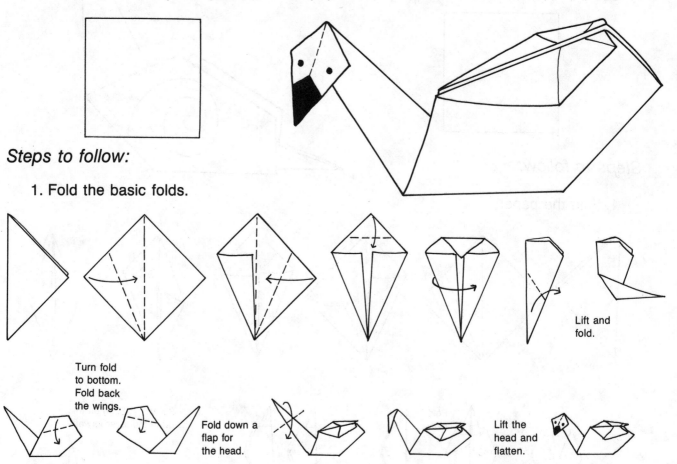

*Steps to follow:*

1. Fold the basic folds.

Turn fold
to bottom.
Fold back
the wings.

Fold down a
flap for
the head.

Lift and
fold.

Lift the
head and
flatten.

2. Add details with crayon or felt pen.

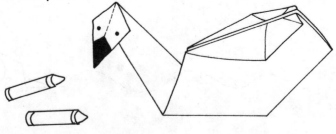

*Uses:*

- Paste the white swan to a 6'' (15cm) black square. Use these squares as a border for a bulletin board displaying students' poetry.
- Paste the swan to a blue sheet of construction paper. Use scraps of paper to add cattails and other pond plants to the picture.

# Frog

### It hops!

## Materials:

Begin with a rectangle. Use a 3'' x 5½'' (7.5 x 14cm) paper for a small frog. Use a 6'' x 11'' (15 x 28cm) paper for a larger frog. Duplicating paper is a workable weight.

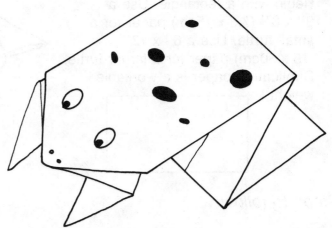

## Steps to follow:

### 1. Fold the paper.

Open again and then fold opposite corner.

Open and push in sides. Press flat.

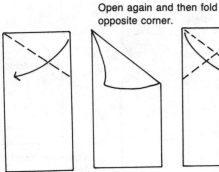 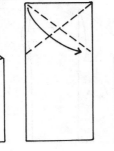 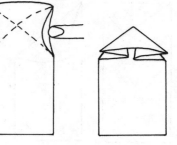

Fold insides.

Fold tips up. Press flat.

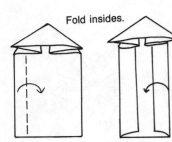 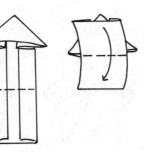

### 2. Color eyes and add details.

Stroke the frog's back gently to make him hop.

## Uses:

- Celebrate the Calaveras Jumping Frog Jubilee in May by making and enjoying these hopping frogs.
- Create a pond scene on the bulletin board. Use blue paper backing and pin green grass around the edge. Add lily pads in the center. Pin frogs on the lily pads.

# Turtle

## Materials:

Begin with a rectangle. Use a 3'' x 6'' (7.5 x 15cm) paper for a small turtle. Use a 6'' x 12'' (15 x 30cm) paper for a larger turtle. Duplicating paper is a workable weight.

## Steps to follow:

### 1. Fold the paper.

Open again and then fold opposite corner.    Open and push in sides. Press flat.

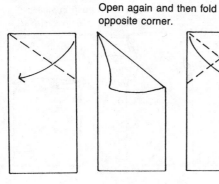

Follow the same steps on bottom.

Fold out the legs.    Fold in tips.    Fold sides back out.

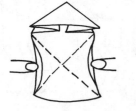 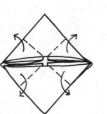 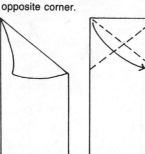 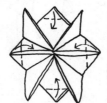 

### 2. Add details with crayon or felt pen.

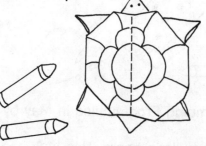

## Uses:

- Attach a string to the turtle and tug on it to pull it along.
- Use these turtles to tell the story of *Rosebud* by Leo Lioni.

Folded Paper Projects